Fingerboarding is a great i
you can achieve the same
landing a new trick. This book covers everything from basic
tricks such as the Ollie and Kickflip, to the more intermediate
tricks and combinations such as a 360 flip to tailslide.

As well as being a fun imitation of the real thing, fingerboarding
is also great for the development of a child's flexibility of the
fingers.

A quick note before we begin
When performing a trick on a tech deck, for many reasons its
not like how you would perform a trick on a real skateboard. For
starters its not a real skateboard and you don't use your feet. Its
more about giving the board a slight flick or pushing the board in
a certain way to cause the board to flip.

Throughout this book the illustrations provided are for a right
handed fingerboarder. The illustrations provided will be in order
from right to left unless otherwise stated, in which case there will
be an arrow to define the direction of the fingerboarder,
alternatively it would be in order by numbers. Also please note
that throughout this book when referring to skating forward, this
actually means skating from right to left for a right handed
fingerboarder.

Disclaimer
This book is in no way endorsed by the tech deck trademark
manufacturer.

Cover image by Philip Platzer- Photocase.com
Fingerboard on halfpipe photo by inkje- Photocase.com
Practicing tricks photo by airportrait- iStock.com
Fingerboard on Chapter page by shoot_nik- iStock
Book design and production by James Mossman
Author Daniel Sleeves/ James Mossman
Illustrations © 2012 James Mossman
Copyright ©2012 James Mossman
Website www.fingerboarder.co.uk

Table of Contents

Terminology

Pop
The term pop is used when referring to popping down the tail or nose of the board to *pop* the board up off the floor.

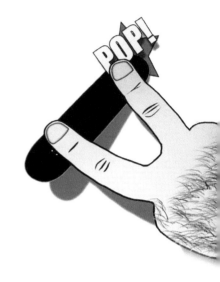

Catch
When referring to catching a board, it means catching the board with your two fingers on the griptape. Not actually catching the board with your hands.

Manual
A manual is where either the back or the front of the board is elevated off the ground whilst moving.

BS and FS
Front Side and Back Side are terms used in skateboarding to decipher between different directions of rotation.

When skating regular, as in with your right hand skating towards the left; A Front Side spin would be when you turn your hand anti-clockwise. A Backside spin is when you would spin your hand clockwise

Back Side

Front Side

Board set up

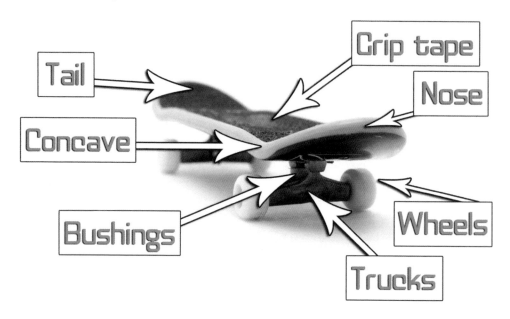

Truck tightness and bushings
The trucks of a skateboard are what holds the wheels which connect to the bottom of the skateboard on what is called a baseplate.

The general rule of thumb is that the loser your trucks, the more your trucks will move around making it easier to turn. This will however, make it hard to perform certain tricks such as the kickflip. This is because your board will be leaning inwards due to the placement of the fingers and make it harder to get the essential flick to make it flip. The tightness of your trucks should all come down to individual preference and what works for you.

Having tight trucks makes your board more stable and solid but will make turns harder compared to loose trucks which can turn more dramatically and sharply.

Concave

The concave of the board is the curve at both the nose and tail of the board. A concave creates more ease when performing tricks compared to a more flat skateboard or in this case a fingerboard. A concave size can vary between manufacturers and the size is all down to individual skater preference. With fingerboards, the size can differ between various manufacturers.

Bushings

The bushings are the two rings that are fitted to the trucks and are designed to provide flexibility for turning.

Nose and tail

The nose and tail of the board depends on the direction in which the skater is skating. So if you are a right handed fingerboarder you would skate towards the left (hereby, throughout this book known as forward), and the nose of the board would be on the left, and the tail at the right. The general rule of thumb for this is that the tail of the board would be at the rear end of the board of the direction to which you are skating.

Griptape

The griptape is the layer of sandpaper on top of the board which is used to give grip to a skateboarder. Unlike a real skateboard which uses a more rugged sandpaper to help shoes grip; the grip tape of a fingerboard is far smoother to help with performing tricks.

Useful Tips

Get a grip- useful tip for gaining grip

Because fingerboards
come with real grip tape,
you may find it hard to
perform tricks.

A useful tip for getting a little extra grip is to simply rub your
fingers on a worktop or wooden surface. By doing this doesn't
mean your fingers will simply stick to the board when you pop
an Ollie, as that would be cheating. But it does get you a little
extra grip.

Ollie Roll back

If you are finding it difficult to learn an Ollie then you may want
to practice by doing an ollie roll back. An ollie roll back is where
you skate forward and when you want to Ollie you would then
roll back in the apposite direction and use the back momentum
to pop up the board.

Basic tricks

Ollie

An Ollie is one of the most basic tricks on a skateboard or fingerboard and is one of the first tricks to master. Many people learning the Ollie place their back finger (the finger used to pop the tail of the board) too far back making it difficult to control the balance of the board and will often cause the board to rotate or flip.

The idea is to place your back finger just where the concave of the tail of the board begins and your front finger at the nose of the board over the inner bolts.

Now apply a little pressure and pop the tail of the board, as you do this pull the board up and level out the front of the board. Try practicing this trick on your leg as previously demonstrated, this will help you get used to the motion of performing an ollie.

A useful tip for learning any trick is to practice on your leg. This is because when you pop the tail of the board on your leg the board will be more inverted than on a flat surface. This will then make it easier to pull up and level the board out to perform an Ollie.

Go on give it a go.

Pop down on the tail of the board

Pull up and level your board out

Land it!

Switch Ollie

A switch Ollie on a fingerboard is when you skate in the opposite direction to how you would normally. It can be a little tricky to learn because you may find it harder to pop the nose of the board with your front (left) finger

Instead of using your back finger to pop the board, as you would do when performing an Ollie. Use your front (left) finger to pop the tail of the board and pull up whilst leveling out your board like you would when performing a regular Ollie.

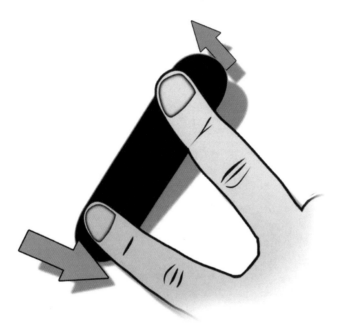

You may find it harder to pop the board off the ground but I often find you don't need to with a switch Ollie.

Nollie

To perform this trick, skate forward as you would normally (from right to left when skating right handed). Now place your front finger at the nose of the board (as shown in the image above) and pop the nose off the ground whilst pulling up with your back finger to lift the board off the ground.

Back side 360 pop shove-it

A back side 360 pop shove-it is where the board spins 360 degrees back side as shown in the images below.

To perform this trick place your front finger over the bolts of the board at around 3/4 the width of the board. Place your back finger hanging slightly over the tail of the concave and pop down whilst sweeping your back finger inwards.

You might find that when you do this the board may flip out so make sure your front finger is flat and slightly over hanging to reduce the chance of flipping.

Make sure you give it enough sweep to rotate the board the full 360 degrees. When done correctly the board should appear to simply rotate around the front finger.

Catch the board..

Land it!

Kickflip

As the name suggests, a Kickflip is a trick performed by kicking your feet off the board. A Kickflip on a fingerboard works on the same principle.

To perform a Kickflip on a fingerboard, place your front finger over the bolts on the right of the nose as shown in the image below. Place your back finger in the standard Ollie position and pop the tail of the board. As you do this, flick your front finger towards your body to make the board flip. Once the board has flipped the full rotation, catch the board and land it.

Try it on a half pipe..

A Kickflip can be very difficult to pull off on a half pipe compared to doing one on a flat surface. It all depends on the angle and verticalness of the quarter pipe.

I will be demonstrating how to perform a Kickflip on a quarter pipe with a slight vert. The idea is to get some air out of the quarter pipe and simply flick the board with your front finger to cause the board to flip. Make sure not to flick the board too hard as it may cause the board to flip away. Now catch the board before it over flips and land back in the quarter pipe.

Heelflip

This trick can be a little tricky to master compared to the Kickflip but a little practice makes perfect.

Place your fingers in a Kickflip position, only this time place your front finger slightly further over the board.

Now instead of popping a Kickflip by flicking your front finger towards your body, stretch your front finger forwards as you pop up the board.

By flicking your finger in such a way should cause the board to flip. Practice this until you get the flick just right to perform a perfect flip.

Varial Kickflip

Place your front finger hanging just over the bottom right bolt at the nose of the board.

Now place your back finger over the right bolts on the concave covering the width of the board.

Apply some pressure and pop down the tail of the board . As you do this, flick your front finger towards your body as you would to perform a Kickflip;

Only this time, use your back finger to give it a little sweep inwards, just as you would when performing a Pop Shove-it.

Once the board has rotated the full 180 degrees, catch the board and land it.

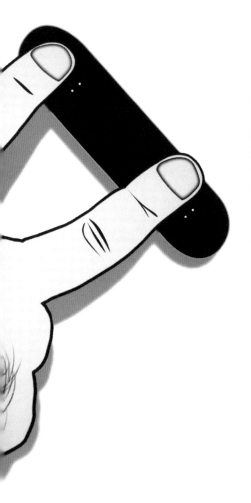

Advanced tricks

Switch Heelflip

Place your back finger on the tail of the board at around half the width of the board. Place your front finger over the bolts on the inside of the nose of the board (refer to image on the left). Make sure your front finger is hanging over the edge just a touch.

Now pop down on the tail of the board and pull up as you would when performing a regular switch Ollie. As you do this, the board should pull up with the back finger having grip on the inner corner of the board . This should cause the board to flip.

Try to keep you front finger as straight as possible to ensure the board flips correctly.

(Images are from left to right) →

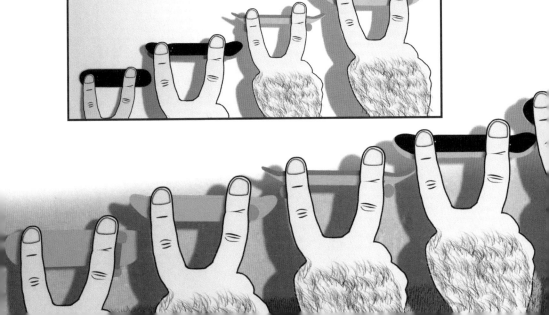

360 Flip

Place your back finger on the tail with the tip of your finger at the corner of the tail concave.

Now place your front finger just before the truck bolts in a Kickflip position hanging half over the board. By having your front finger in this position will cause the board to flip like a Kicklflip.

Apply a little pressure and pop the tail of the board whilst sweeping your tail finger inwards to create rotation.

Practice this until you make the correct rotation and flip, catch the board and role away clean.

(illustration continues on the following page)

Flick Off

Hardflip

To perform a hardflip, I would suggest you get your pop shove-its and kickflips mastered.

Set up your fingers like how you would for a kickflip and pop down the tail of the board. As you do this, pull your finger back to make the board inverted.

As you do this, use your back finger to push the board to create rotation like how you would when performing a pop shove-it. As the board rotates, simply catch the board

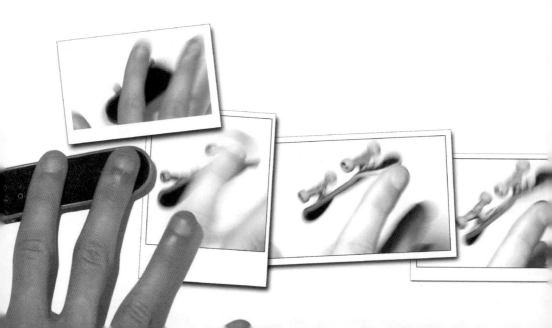

Grind tricks

So now that you've mastered the Ollie, you want to get some grinds in your bag of tricks. Grind tricks are quite simple to perform once you've mastered the Ollie so I will only guide you through the first couple.

50-50 Grind

The first grind to try out would be the 50-50 grind. A 50-50 grind is where both trucks are on a rail or edge of the ledge. Its the simplist grind to learn. Approach the ledge or rail, pop an Ollie and grind the obstacle, pop off the end and land.

50-50 Grind

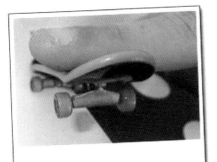

5-0 Grind

5-0 Grind

A 5-0 grind is where only the back truck is on the rail or ledge and the front truck is lifted off the ground, much like how you would do a manual.

Nose Grind

Performing a nose grind is when the front trucks of the skateboard grinds along a ledge or rail whilst the tail of the board is elevated off the ground.

Nose Grind

Tail Slide

Tail Slide
A tailslide is where the tail of the board slides along a ledge or rail.

All you need to do is approach the ledge or rail so that it is front of you and pop an Ollie. As you do this add a front side 90° spin, land the tail of the board on the ledge and slide.

Pop out, land it and cruise away.

Nose Slide
A nose slide is just like a tailslide only as the name would suggest, you would slide using the nose of the board

Nose Slide

Blunt Slide

Bluntslide
To perform a Bluntslide you need to approach and Ollie over a ledge or rail, then land the tail of the board on the obstacle and slide.

Nose Bluntslide
To perform a nose bluntslide you need to approach and Ollie with a 90 degree front side spin over a ledge or rail, then land the nose of the board on the obstacle and slide.

Nose Blunt Slide

Crooked Grind

Crooked Grind
A crooked grind is where you perform a grind with the nose of the board at a crooked angle, hence the name "crooked grind".

Over Crooked Grind
An over crooked grind is just like a regular crooked grind only this time you would pop the tail of the board over the ledge or rail.

Over Crooked Grind

Salad Grind

This trick is quite simular to a 5-0 grind. To perform a salad grind simply ollie onto the ledge or rail. Now, instead of landing how you would for a 5-0, land with the back trucks firmly on the ledge and have the nose of the board hanging over.

Salad Grind

Smith Grind

Smith Grind

A smith grind is where the back trucks are on the ledge or rail and the front of the board would be hanging down

Combination tricks- flips with grinds
Kickflip to tailslide
To achieve this trick you first need to master the kickflip which we previously learnt from this book. But this time add a 90 degree rotation. Make sure you get enough height though. After all, you do need to land the tail of the board on a ledge or rail.

In this case it will be a ledge, pop a kickflip and get the 90° rotation, now catch the board and slam the tail of the board onto the ledge. This may take you a while to learn and you may find yourself constantly pushing the board away as you try to catch the board. Try to get the flip as close to the ledge as possible, so when you do catch the board you can slap the tail straight onto the ledge.

Slide for a bit and snap off the ledge and skate away.

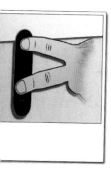

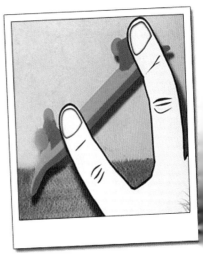

270° flip to tailslide
Approach a ledge or rail at a 30° angle whilst set up in a 360 flip position.

Get close enough to the ledge and perform a 360 flip, as you do this, move your back finger towards the ledge and catch the board on its rotation at a 270 spin. Slam the tail of the board on the ledge and slide, pop off the ledge 90° and roll away clean.

...or you could always add a flip off the edge to spice things up.

Household fingerboard spots

Some of the best spots for fingerboards is within the comfort of your very own home...

Sinks
Be careful though as it may form scratches and upset mum and dad!

Sink

You've been warned!

Window ledge

Window ledge
Try doing some tricks off your kitchen window ledge and landing on the worktop.

Stack of DVD's

Books and DVD cases
Stack up some DVD's or some books and bust some tricks!

Fireplace
Fireplaces often have little ledges that you can do grinds and tricks off.

Fire place

Make sure its not on or you might catch fire!

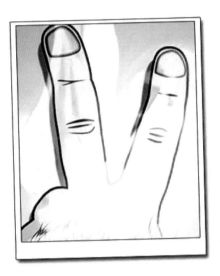

Get creative and make something yourself!
The best thing about fingerboarding is creating your own skate spots. So get some cardboard, some scissors, some sellotape and get creative!

Conclusion

Remember practice makes perfect. A lot of these tricks will, much like real skateboarding, require a lot of practice to master so don't get worked up if you can't land it right away. Just have fun with it and before you know it, you will be a master on a fingerboard

So to cap it off, I hope you enjoyed this book and please feel free to get in contact if you have any questions.

Keep locked on to updates, competitions and special offers by signing up to the newsletter at www.fingerboarder.co.uk

Sign up to the fingerboard newsletter for competitions and fresh new content

www.fingerboarder.co.uk

Index

Sign up to the fingerboard newsletter for competitions and fresh new content

www.fingerboarder.co.uk

46408318R00018

Made in the USA
Lexington, KY
02 November 2015